2/16

D0746463

DISCARD

THE TANGLED LINE

CANARIUM BOOKS

ANN ARBOR, IOWA CITY, SHANGHAI

SPONSORED BY
THE UNIVERSITY OF MICHIGAN
CREATIVE WRITING PROGRAM

THE TANGLED LINE

TOD MARSHALL

To Tar —
w/ admiration —
Rock Chalk!
Tod
11/16/2011

Canarium Books
Ann Arbor, Iowa City, Shanghai
www.canariumbooks.org

The editors gratefully acknowledge the
University of Michigan Creative Writing Program
for editorial assistance and generous support.

First edition

Printed in the United States of America

CONTENTS

I

II

III

I

DESCRIBE KFC TO ICARUS

Admit the labyrinth, accept
       chicken bones
            piling up in the kitchen—

          to find one feather in all those buckets,
              one feather among the fat and batter

and flesh,
      one feather
         and I'll start the gluing and waxing,

the climbing with a song toward sun.

The ground gives a push. Rocks applaud,
and nearby, waterfalls like rivers of joyful tears—
that time laughing so hard at my son
toddling around the house
with an erection on which he'd hung
the friendship bracelet from the Bible People
that said "What Would Jesus Do?"
Answer that one and you might be able to see
those purples, reds, and yellows
the subtle lavender gloss, sheeny pinks,
even the over-the-top oranges,
and not be tempted to pick the explosive petals
to press into a notebook
with the desperate hope
you could one day open the pages
and say *as it was, so it shall be*. Try again,
write scribbles of smoke against the sky—
fillyum trillium birdfoot violet blueflag.
Try paintbrush, buttercup, try please. Try
fire and tears. Try greeny green green.

DESCRIBE TURNER TO MLK

I

The weight of my son
          at the emergency room
       for an eye injury, sack of flour, sack of salt,
           dusty bag of bones
              collapsed

                      after all those tears.

       Why does Turner
        come to mind,
             those shackled ankles,
       those drowning slaves?

II

And horizons.
        Each measure, each cleaving
of flesh to soil, breath to sentence, body
           toward earth. The shepherd
          watches his flock
            cross the stream;
         nymphs bathe and flirt
      and sun themselves on rocks. Water
            against ankles, pebbles
              beneath feet.

III

An old woman sits next to us,
                    and every time she shifts
              in her seat,
                         I can hear her bones click.
     Dying,
              her faulty architecture
                    like an old radiator,
                         cooling engine.

IV

The burden
              of seeing, explosive sunlight,
       the swirling painted water
                    pouring over Turner's slaves.
                                   My son
                         sleeps. Have you ever walked
                              out
                                   into the sticky heat
              of a Memphis night
                    and asked for gunshots
                         to stop for just one hot hour?
     O heap of body, heap of bones,
                    heap of dreams, heap of moans.

V

A story with a happy ending
        and no answers,
                slight corneal scratch
             healed with anti-bacterial rinse,
        the eyeball's protective pocket
                cupping the universe
           like a calm inlet
                    offering a foundering ship
                        protection from rough seas. You tell me:
What washes blood from a balcony?
I'm listening. I'm saying *please*.
        The sun rises quickly.
        And so do sea monsters.

APPROACHING MEMPHIS,
CHOIR IN THE BACKGROUND

After hanging wings on his son,
he cried like rain on the plowman's furrows,

showers on the river delta, flash flood
up to the stilted porch. He knew that fusion

of music and light: when wax melts,
the song ends, hot jelly on the boy's flesh.

Asked for wisdom, say grandfather dies,
father dies, child dies, the natural order of things.

Asked for song, listen to waves carrying
feathers across the ocean, melted wax

like peanut butter on a blue plate. Leave the refrain
to that gold record, the sun: oh child, we can stay

on the island without any wings, we can walk
along the beach and watch the frantic gulls,

catch crayfish for dinner, you within arm's reach.
We can ignore the gyrating wind whispering,

Don't be cruel, the boy will soar closer and closer.

DESCRIBE DIVORCE TO MARTINIS

Would Jerry Lewis declare the gray sky blue?
Not the heavy telethon host, but the slapstick spasm

for whom you felt pity to give in and laugh.
Would he agree that even the ugliest scars grow smooth,

become bearable hours in an empty house, the answer
to where does your son sometimes sleep?

Ask the comedians where laughter ends up living after the split,
the meaning of a pocketful of toothpicks and olives;

ask them to repeatedly perform their slapstick routines
until the universe is shaken and stirred

into a tolerable concoction that seems suave
and smooth but burns the gut like swallowed bleach.

Better yet, ask Jerry to rise from some farcical flop on the floor
and pour another drink for Dean, staggering Dean, charming Dino

slurring each syllable as if no sound should ever be alone. In fact,
make it two. I'll have whatever the guy in the tux is drinking.

THE SHORE

I discovered the body, finally.
Salt water dissolved feathery wax,
fish had picked at pale skin, eyes

long gone, flying
with sharp-beaked gulls, I guess.
Those who say it's a myth of foolish boys

know nothing of fathers: his shoulder blades
curved like sea shells
when he hunched over a bowl of cereal

slurping the milk. Would a seal-skin boat
have served us? Would we have starved
at sea? Those who deride ambition

know nothing of sky. Ships,
plowmen in the fields,
only offer rumor and innuendo, a lack

of facts. The sun witnesses everything,
and although some claim indifference,
I know better. A father sobs

drops of light,
and the sun knows this language,
vocabulary that ignites the earth.

DESCRIBE CUSTODY TO OMELETS

Which means,
probably,
to begin without the convention of a sentence—
                                    the trees were

                    ocean
teasing sand
                                    the elk at the edge of the clearing

or

                    threatened that I would never see my child again
                            a friend said that they
                        were just words—
maple tree tipping toward sun
                    ash colored sky
                                    peeled back

to a starry spread

                                            bright red skin
                                and then the white streak
                        of a strap
            where cloth

                        lied to light.

Just
                    is enough. Granite.
                        Birch. Beloved.
                                In my *National Geographic Atlas*
the haughty pose of the mercenaries

reveals a distrust about getting paid
about the payoff
the transfer of this for that.

And when the birds land

on my window ledge

I whisper to them

through glass:
"Watch those eggs.
You may never see them again."

DAEDALUS BECOMES A DADAIST
AT THE DENTIST

Ha, ha, ho, ho, he says to the nurse.
Roof canal, he mutters and nods
out the window to the drain gutter.

She smiles and says numbness
usually comes in a few minutes.
Hee, hee. I thaw eh toolk years.

The dentist has seen incisors like these,
a crown on the third molar,
inflammation, gum disease, soft pulp.

Bite this,
he says, inserting cotton gauze; he prods and pokes;
he scrapes. Now spit and rinse.

Nothing we eat is sweeter than guilt,
the dentist says. Out the window
drills swirl holes in sky.

DESCRIBE BRETON TO THE ENLIGHTENMENT

It's not a manifesto, really.
Never a declaration of drawers. Nothing to
    break, only the delicate saucer
                        on the kitchen counter
that's filled with yesterday's milk,
the best of all
possible cream.

Reactionary's the middle name of guillotine;
revolution woven into the executioner's rope.

The many wide-eyed girls of Oklahoma
squint when they read it.

And in Texas, prairie dogs
vouch for order, dig tunnels to elude the moon
lording over the night air.

On the Kansas plains,
rattlesnakes slither along, strike slow vermin,
and slumber with half-
digested rats
quivering against poison.

Cacti
bare pricklies to the moon,

and hunched buzzards wait,
pink heads like nauseated light bulbs.

Dead meat always arrives.

Art in a powdered wig
        means time for murder.

DESCRIBE FLY FISHING
TO MARIE ANTOINETTE

Regulations say
>> the tragic grace
>>>> of catch and release. We poach:

elk hair masquerading as antennae or wings,
>> and the water—a sweet stretch on the Coeur d'Alene
>>>> where cutthroat rise like children

kissing the belly of heaven. Hunger
>> imagines the center of plenty,
>>>> and movement—the shimmy of insects,

flounder of dying flies—is revolutionary truth.
>> The whoosh of line
>>>> inscribes infinity loops;

drift of river pulls the fly above
>> hungry fish. Water executes all.
>>>> On the ridge, six elk graze

huckleberry shrubs to lacy tatters.
>> They save their bugling for fall
>>>> when hatches last through cool afternoons.

With pomp, Marie announces
>> that she loves the cutthroat
>>>> most, declares elk hair real.

Who do we fool?
>> We float. Who do I
>>>> fool? Ripples expose the lies.

DESCRIBE MANIFEST DESTINY
TO HIGH MODERNISM

Waking to white mountains,

      toothy music, a soothing

settling into the saddle,

          or long strides through the twiggy landscape

of a fading painting,

      Meriwether Lewis

         despairing

           in Tennessee.

Wagons whisper

      through sand, prairie schooners stuck

near stacks

        of buffalo skin and barrels of tongue

to sing the blues

      of Meriwether Lewis

         like nothing else

           from here to Tennessee.

WHAT THE AGE DEMANDED

Chicken-necked Daedalus will stew
        for days and gloom around
the house, asking dying plants, new
        photos on the wall, a mound

of unopened mail: "What did I do
        wrong?" As if forgiveness
seeped and flowed through the thirsty roots
        of aloe leaves, as if blessings

would unfold from an envelope,
        as if the penance of portraits
("Icarus with Clouds") grew hope.
        He knows that he made a bet,

and the boy was a necessary loss,
        what happens when you fly,
expendable. O Daedalus,
        don't try to hide in a sigh.

Your legacy's ensured: maze maker,
        inventor's patron, you cad.
No one will mistake you for father,
        no one will call you dad.

DESCRIBE DADA TO NAPOLEON

Waterloo, waterloo, water loo loo loo.

More often than not
disease and rot
will kill your men
again and again.

So feed them well
and watch their feet.

Soldiers should always wash their feet.
Soldiers should always wash their feet.
People will always wash their hands.
People will always wash their hands.

Waterloo, waterloo, water loo loo loo.
Waterloo, waterloo, water loo loo loo.

Gather the tatters of bodies
out of the frenzied cataract of life
out of the letters spelling 'forest'
steps the forest with its treetops and wild sows

out of soil out of sandy loam
out of hard channeled rock
from deep beneath the surface
plumes squirt toward sky.

What for you what for you what for you and me.
Water loo, water loo, water loo loo loo
Water loo.

You are necessary.

You are the new you.

You combine art and electricity, ham and rye.

You are the sharp mustard between meat and cheese.

You cling like burdock, flow like river. You are to your like we to wet.

You house builder you state builder you democracy builder extreme.

You hang sheetrock with neat seams.

You paint the scenery so it seems real.

You plumb. You deep deep deep.

You wire the stars. You roof the sky.

You intelligent, brave, brilliant, honest, you risk taker extreme.

O risky risky you.

You move, you muse, you dazzle, you brilliant. Brilliant, brilliant you.

You genius, you incarnation, you epiphany, Virgin Mary in moldy bread.

You Walt Whitman mixed with Martin Luther King.

You Dickinson, Shakespeare, Dante's lost brother.

You Rome. You Byzantium.

You Marconi, you radio, you chat room, you needed.

You flag. You necessary. O say can you.

DESCRIBE DAISY CUTTERS TO ORPHEUS

The monarch in the front yard
floats like a shred of tiger,
rising and dropping to the score
of piano keys popcorn-played,

something by Chopin a young girl
practices diligently
in the sunbeams of a bay window—
other children riding bikes

through the shouty afternoon—to strengthen
her fingers and to learn the lesson
that endurance can lead to grace. The dying
Bengal tiger at the Kabul Zoo

roused people to send checks
in envelopes with return addresses
so postal clerks wouldn't suspect anthrax.
The girl's classmate grows fingernails

long as religious tracts, sometimes scratches her arms
in rosy rows that turn to scab-black stripes.
Last summer, two hundred and fifty million butterflies
froze into notes floating in the wind.

Are your fingers sore from practice?
Is one nail ragged from chewing, another long and pointy
like a pale cavefish never to see the world?
Lure it to the surface. Look through its eyes:

a monarch's unruly music
roars across the tops of daisies, the flaccid fish
flopping
in the dust, wishing darkness back, wishing

caves, its skeleton a reliquary of a new religion
that's already begun.

II

DAEDALUS RETIRES

Evel Knievel's last stunt:
jump the Mississippi near the Desoto Bridge
on a souped-up motorcycle from which,
halfway across, he'll leap into the sky
and rise higher on waxy wings and chicken feathers
to swoop down into adoration in Arkansas.
He recruits Daedalus as technical advisor
(ignoring the hesitant letters of recommendation),
researches Desoto's brutal march
from Florida to Mississippi
(inspiring conquest),
visits the balcony where Martin got shot
(a fellow revolutionary),
and hangs out at the Pyramid
surrounded by reporters and fans
where he asks, "Why did pyramids
go out of style?" The Mississippi is a mile wide.
Daedalus tells Evel to watch the altimeter,
to switch to feathers at the exact apex,
to trust them to glide him to shore.
Evel poses in red, white, and blue
for photographs in front of the silver pyramid
where he says, "Those Egyptians
could have learned something from steel."
They steamroll housing projects
to build a runway three miles long,
tell tenants that this is about mythology

not privilege. "Crazy white folks
doing crazy shit," some mutter,
aware of how history bulldozes
the same people again and again.
Evel Knievel revs the bike for hours.
Some speculate he's gone chicken,
Snake River broke his will,
say he's heard the scuttle about Icarus,
but then, *varoooom*,
the motorcycle screams by Beale Street
where a drunk passed out in the gutter
dreams of God in a rocket,
Evel's white fringe flapping in the wind
as he launches over muddy water
with gusto, with confidence, with verve:
they never find the sunken motorcycle,
and because the glider swoops into Arkansas
downstream from the intended landing pad,
the press reports are late, reliant on rumors
from the crowd splayed out for miles
on the western shore: some witnesses
describe Pentecostal fire, some
recount a fluffy white cloud
with tidings of a New Kingdom,
some say they touched an old man in white leather
before he limped off into the sunset.
Back in Tennessee, reporters clamor for interviews,
but the cagey Greek inventor ducks the spotlight,
even declines an intimate sit-down with Oprah

to help fans understand the depth of his loss,
how he spends every day
missing his boy. He retires instead
to Spokane, and although he'll never
sleep easy, he occasionally smiles
because he knows that he lifted
a reckless man into the holy land of Arkansas
wearing a white cape that was, according to one report,
found near Fayetteville and displayed in City Hall,
a crowd lining up on Saturdays
to touch the dusty cloth
and feel the fabric of life in the sky.

HATCH

Mayflies—
tiny white smudges
above blue sky

reflected in the creek
until wings get wet
and useless

except
to flutter recklessly
and attract

the attention of teeth.

COST OF ADMISSION

Vertebrae strewn among juniper and sage,

a three-foot length of spine tinseled with strands of grizzled meat,

bleached pelvis like a tribal mask,

one femur, a skull with two rows of blunt teeth and empty orbs for horns.

Owls and rattlesnakes gorge on mice

and voles that reproduce prolifically because they're stupid, slow, and tasty.

Coyotes yip and howl, snarl and shred

the rib cage, leave raccoon and raven to pick whitening bones.

At last, even the black beetles abandon

the skeleton, scratchy trails scribing a maze beneath barbed wire

stretching north and south.

If it could, hunger would eat the sun.

ADMIT CIRCUMFERENCE TO ARRIVAL

Where snow starts to fall and branches crackle
with ice, the air whispers failure.
The remaining fact: his jacket was not warm.

After that, it's all conjecture.
His old boots left prints for maybe an hour,
depending on the first flakes, how fast

they fell. I'll guess the note was pinned
to a lapel, that his glasses dropped as he slumped
against a trunk, sipping his flask, saving

one last drink. And then dusk overpowered
birch trees, made branches dance the dance
of shadows, and probably that's when the snow

fell harder, flakes large as stars slowly floating
to join the hard pack of the forest floor.
He must have laughed, my great grandfather—

six kids left in the middle of the Depression,
no end in sight—as he finished the whiskey
and spoke his name clearly, loudly,

into the oncoming dark,
settling against the rough bark, proposing
a toast, the deepening snow.

NO NIGHTINGALES IN KANSAS

Always on the dirt roads outside of El Dorado,
my epileptic uncle drove too fast in winter: fuck the sun, he'd say—
pushing the speedometer to seventy, cottonwoods blurring
into mesmerizing spindles of streaky light—
screw the cops, the cold, and the wind,
piss on the president and rich pricks with shit-eating grins,
fuck the moon, the bills, the deer, and the stars,
and then he'd skid to a stop through gravelly sand and snow,
and we'd smoke a bowl,
and midnight would gather like a black hole beneath the pickup's cab,
his head slumped against the driver's window, and for a few hours
he'd sleep, a child returned to the drowsy numbness of a mother's hand,
and I'd stare at him to augur
why those wide plains and reckless stakes,
why disco and Izod and Reagan,
why speed equaled V-8s floored and roaring
and something to snort when the teacher looked away,
why that shuttle couldn't at least have orbited for a few quiet hours,
and why the weight of arrival always fell toward Wichita
and the mazy cul-de-sacs of suburban streets,
why *2112* and Ayn Rand (our music loud and deep), and why I loved him
(falling stoned to sleep),

and then we'd wake freezing
buried beneath two inches of newly fallen snow:
fuck the dawn, the ice, the clouds,
piss on the sky and all those bare trees,

fuck an A, a B, and a C, he'd say as he spun out, gravel and ice pluming
    from rear tires,
and tore down country roads, past dinosaur wells ca-chunking,
    ca-chunking,
mini clocks measuring consumption divided by speed
against the prime number called horizon, called this spinning planet,
called the weariness, the fever, and the fret, past farmhouses
where men lumbered through pre-dawn chores,
women fixing omelets in kitchens lit by one bare bulb,
cracked egg shells piled in the sink,
and he'd slide to a stop, gotta take a freakin' leak,
and cows in the field
would look at us pissing yellow ribbons,
spelling our names with cursive lines in the vast white,
and he would run at them waving wild arms,
and I'd follow, climbing the barbed wire fence, kicking up drifts,
hearts destined for the slaughterhouse,
intent to scream not like meat but the blade.

MEANWHILE

On the great plains,
           water troughs
hoard rain against heat

that slips gold into wheat stalks
           with a long
invisible kiss. Cattle gather

at this silver ring near the shoulder
           of Highway 50
that also draws from the windmill's

clattering pump, and when pick-ups
           swoosh
beyond barbed wire, they raise

their heads for a second,
           then return
to slurping, a quick nod

that signals gratitude for water
           and the sharp
pleasure of the salt lick.

ADMIT POSSESSION TO RENT

We stopped at a farmer's house
before parking at the dock
that creaked over the river.
Rowboats for rent, five bucks
an hour, twenty for the day.
Deep water: I knew a canvas bag

was in the trunk. I knew lunch
would be roast beef sandwiches
and hot stew from a thermos,
chunks of carrot and potatoes
cut by my mother who slept
through the racket of our leaving.

While my father paid, I loaded
the boat with our poles
and tackle boxes, lead sinkers
shaped like grey pears, raincoats
and a case of beer. I was ten
and I knew my dad would toss

that canvas bag into the aluminum
boat with a thunk. We *fish for gar*
with kittens, he'd yelled last night
at my mother, and that was that.
The rowboat slid from the dock,
the occasional clunk of the first

six-pack clipped on the fish stringer,
and I knew that I should take my time
fastening the wire leader
to the brass swivel, tying on
those massive sinkers. I knew
that the six-inch treble hook

would tremble in my hands,
and when I was done, I knew
what came next, a canvas bag,
stiff kittens, blood. I tore
two hooks through the side
of a calico, yanked upward with a

sharp tug to lodge the third barb
beneath the ribs. I dangled
my fingers in cold water
to wash them, then reared
the rod back into a cast that splashed
twenty feet from the boat.

He popped the third beer and finished
baiting his hook. Too deep
for an anchor, we drifted,
and far beneath, the gar cruised
back and forth, their prehistoric
snouts slicing the dark, bumping

our bait again and again
until that fierce hunger I was learning
said clamp down and take it.

MEANWHILE

High desert
        coulee
near the banks

of a spring
        creek
prickly Hawthorne trees

surround
        hollowed out
copses

where scrawny black
        bears
leave piles of scat

decorated with dazzling
        indigestible
red berries.

The owl spooks before we cross the creek.
In its grove, the tiniest bones you'll ever see.
Mushrooms in the spoor, thorny locust trees
all around. Cougar tracks announce: be meek.

Walking home we find a deer skull, sun-bleached
teeth in u-shaped rows, once an *ungulate grazing.*
Dusk. The owl who-whos over sage and cheat-
grass. Mice tremble. They fear what's coming.

ADMIT TIME TO SPACE

Five children posed in a two-tiered group—

wide polyester lapels, zippers, and bright labyrinthine patterns that echo
　　　　nothing in nature—

the oldest brother's bruised ribs hidden beneath a corduroy blazer,
　　　　the eldest sister forgetting when the flash goes off

what happened in the basement, a middle sister's scar where the ceramic
　　　　ashtray smacked her.

You get the idea. When the photographer says "Smile!" we do.

Hang the portrait in the living room and serve cold cuts at the family
　　　　reunion.

Decorate the huge house of the self.

The glass will still get dusty, the paper yellow and bleach in the sun.

Slide out the group shot and slip in a landscape, furrowed fields, rusty
　　　　tractor beside

white chickens or back-dropped by pines. Same difference.

The gaps between the trees, the teeth.

MEANWHILE

Piles of bear scat by the creek:

aftermath of scavenging crayfish
and mussels from the muddy bottom
(gorged bowels roar for relief),

or to claim this pool near the clear spring
as private drinking trough of *ursus americanus*,
sacred well so cool and deep?

Or that the spindly spine of basalt to the east
frames a sunrise
like no other place on the high desert,

bears reveling in scenery,
claws on those massive smelly paws
shrinking for a brief while,

teeth in long snouts,
those huge jaws, no longer compelled
to snap bones, crush shells, chomp

trout in half with one bite,
instead relaxed as the bears squat
and sigh, inhale the last bluish black of night,

bid the stars goodbye,
and calmly do their beary-business?
Sunrise breaks over sharp rock

and frosty sage burns with silvery fire.
That it could be true, this outhouse
as a soothing balm in the desert,

that the peace that passeth understanding
and a bear shitting in the woods
were equally probable.

STILL MORE WORK

The beetles bust their asses for days,
stripping flesh from the dead cow,
this overtime shift they didn't request
but had to take. No one's in charge
but the sun. Every now and then a crow
carries a brother beetle from the bones
high enough to glimpse mountains and the city
where we scavenge the hide of hours,
skeleton of days. Forget us.
This is about cows with broken legs,
the long rot, coyotes, hawks, and beetles,
with mandibles like opposable thumbs,
a complete kit for taking bodies
apart. Black lords of sage and hunger and dust,
O how they labor in the heat, they know
neither meek nor might, they feed,
they lie on ribs, they creep across skull and hips and spine,
and when nothing's left, dutiful members
of the brutal union that trades hours for food,
they crawl to death's next shift.

THE READER IS URGED
NOT TO READ THIS POEM

What was a garden:
a few green onion shoots,

four persistent peonies
spreading white petals

like baked fish flesh,
red and yellow tulips

blooming early with sudden color,
a bed of purple irises

waving in the wind for an afternoon
then burning beneath the August sun,

and one huge rhubarb,
thick-stalked, broad-leaved,

sour and delicious
in the corner of the yard.

LOAM

Love is peasant. Love is find. It lends me, it is unlike toast, it is prow. It is ride, not self-seeding, it is easy language, it keeps sandy loam close. Love does not spite but rejoices chartreuse, celebrates brindle, cheers wildflower bloom. Love always process, always trout, always whistle and flute, always always very dear. Three remain: grain, hap, and love. And the greatest of these, my brothers and sisters, is love, always peasant, always prow, always sandy loam and always, always near.

A FATHER MUMBLES

You are not lost. I know where you eat and sleep.
Here's news: this summer I grew a garden,

but only half the seeds became blooms, vegetables to keep.
The other stems rose but never blossomed, a sad choir

in the backyard, swaying and singing the garbled music
of dying things. You ate cereal at our kitchen table

with the sloppy energy of snowmelt rushing down
a mountain slope, your shoulder blades angling beneath

a white T-shirt. When I turn soil with my hands,
I remember what does not blossom here

may blossom elsewhere, and be just as beautiful.
And if I said that was solace, the lie would not be untrue.

THE CHOIR AGAIN

Gather ye may
Gather body and shadow and casting of shadows
Gather ye bodies while ye may

Gather hills and pines
Gather the hesitant step toward water
Gather water while ye may

Gather the hills the dust the sky
Gather wind and clouds
Gather hands that pull a body that hold a body
Gather a body
Gather a body you may

Gather water
Gather the breaking surface
Gather we wake and breathe and sleep
Gather shadows burning stone

Gather ripples and feathers
Gather bones

III

THE BOOK OF FAILED DESCRIPTIONS

Myth is prison, a palace,
truth without fact.

Myth is birth and pleasure, teeth and death,
      sharp shiver of that which is broken.

Myth is patriarchal and worn,
      full of fratricide and rape.

Myth is a garden, makes good television,
      memoir,
      the scandal of animals
      and people
      coupling beneath the stars.

Myth is crow eating roadkill and dodging the occasional cars,
      a pile of guts and bones.

Myth is carrying the body back to the den.

                —Close your eyes and count to ten.

1.

"In language, there are always two."

The Iliad
stolen from Thoreau's cabin,
the only thing taken
during those years.
Remember, too, *The Aenied*
(we all have lived
through times of war)
and that passage
a friend said to know well,
"Learn fortitude and toil from me, my son,
Ache of true toil. Good fortune learn from others."

2.

Ultrasound images of my heart.
That it moves and moves
and then moves again,
plump muscle
shuddering, laboring
to make up for one bad valve.

Spots in the ocean
where nothing lives
and yet there is movement,
water moving.

I stand in the river
fishing and watching an osprey
slide through the air
ten feet above the water.

I hear those wings.

3.

Eleven years of loving
can't just vanish. I have photographs.
I have facts. "Hapy Birthday
Dady" scribbled on a card.

> How easy to sit at a desk
> and not see the full moon
> through the window.

> Roy Sullivan, Virginia Park Ranger,
> struck by lightning seven times,
> kills himself after being dumped by a lover.

> "Present fears are less than horrible imaginings."

A friend asks, "Why are you hiding in myth?"

4.

I gather a lock of his hair,
a scrap of T-shirt, a baby tooth,
his tiny spoon, a diaper pin with a blue plastic stork,
the quilted blanket, his first steps,
hands clutching my fingers, the long night
when his fever rose toward 104°,
his split lip at age six when he jumped with outspread
arms, the first shoe, a locket with a toddler photo,
first day of school, first finger painting,
the green cardboard sculpture
like something shaped by Breton, T-ball
games, the flopping trout he squeezed too hard,
his first broken bone, his fear when he felt
my trembling hands trying to tell him
something about the sun.

5.

Trout with a slashed back
.where talons tore dorsal flesh
and the fish slipped
from an osprey's grip
to a lucky landing
in the creek's waiting water,
thrashing and calming,
lingering beneath a deep cutbank,
and weeks later,
taking my elk hair caddis
and leaping
completely out of the water.

On the far bank, a muskrat
struggles and does a melodramatic gangster fall
into the creek where it splashes
and sinks. "Rattlesnake,"
my friend says, and I nod
and stare at where the ripple
swirls into the current

and think about sinking bones.

6.

The court acknowledges the petitioner's long involvement with
_____'s life and sincerely hopes that the parties involved
will have the generosity and wisdom to honor that relationship.

Do not blame the wind
that scatters apple blossoms
ruthlessly. Allow that flowers
desire farewell blessings
before their time has come.

7.

Fishing in the desert creek
a few days after the hearing,
I find bones, steer skulls
with round sockets for horns,
and step near three rattlesnakes,
almost grab a fourth
when climbing a steep bank.
The snakes were sluggish, though,
late spring when the temperatures
in the desert dipped into the thirties
at night. Only one rattled,
and the rain of the previous days
made the fishing terrible, water brown
and swift. I didn't get a bite
and drove home, bought
a bucket of fried chicken,
and ate in front of the television,
his clothes still hanging in a closet.

8.

There is no
end to the hours
when cedars and peaks
scratch the sky's belly.
No garden,
but sometimes, wildflowers.
Sometimes, fish hold against
the river's current
then dart with a silvery
flash downstream.
Sometimes, deer
on the other shore
stand still
for a moment,
then hunch toward
their grazing.

9.

A birthday party and he'll have nothing to do with the inflatable
castle rented and set up on the lawn, only wants to run all
afternoon, playing chase, tag-like game where I growl and laugh
and lumber around the playground, his giggling, both of us
laughing and roaring, and I catch him and he gets away and
climbs to the top of the jungle gym where he looks at me with
worry, and I know that the game is on break, that this is real, and
I walk beneath him and he doesn't pause. He jumps into my
arms, and I catch him.

10.

Ready or not
        here I come——

A feather floats downstream,

the rings of a ripple smooth.

Love is possible. The heron

hunts in shallows with slow

deliberate steps, startles

from the creek, and rises.

Sunlight warms basalt walls

fields of sage, and Hawthorne

groves, here, where tumble-

weeds rove for home.

NOTES

DESCRIBE DADA TO NAPOLEON:

"gather the tatters of bodies ... treetops and wild sows" from André Breton's *Mad Love*, translated by Mary Ann Caws (Bison Books, 1988).

THE BOOK OF FAILED DESCRIPTIONS:

"In language there are always two," Master Deshimaru, quoted by Donald Revell in *Arcady*, (Wesleyan University Press, 2002).

"Learn fortitude and toil from me, my son, / Ache of true toil. Good fortune learn from others" from Robert Fitzgerald's translation of *The Aeneid* (Random House, 1981). A friend's letter highlighted this passage.

"Present fears are less than horrible imaginings." *Macbeth*.

ACKNOWLEDGMENTS

Gratitude to the editors of the following journals, in which versions of these poems first appeared: *The Canary*, *Colorado Review*, *Denver Quarterly*, *Interim*, *High Desert Journal*, *Iowa Review*, *Poetry East*, *Shenandoah*, *Smartish Pace*, and *The Southern Review*.

"Describe Ethics to Wildflowers" and "Describe Custody to Omelets" were reprinted in *Long Journey: Contemporary Northwest Poets* (Oregon State University Press, 2006).

Thanks to the Washington Artist Trust for a Grants for Artist Project award and an Artist Trust Fellowship, both of which helped make this writing possible.

And many thanks also to the editors at Canarium Books for their editorial sense and generous hearts; to Dennis, Scott, Don, and Marshall—good readers, better friends; to the Lorinda Knight Gallery for permission to use *Interior*; to Ryan for artistic vision and kindred sense of adventure.

And most of all, to mom and dad, brothers and sisters—love all of you; to Lincoln ("what falls away is always"); to Henry ("this shaking keeps me steady"); and to Amy (you keep sandy loam close).